ANIMAL ANCESTORS

Written and illustrated by Jon Hughes

Contents

ANIMALS FROM ANOTHER TIME

Can you imagine a world with horses the size of small dogs, whales that walk, and birds that are 10 feet tall? They all lived on Earth at some time in the last 60 million years. They are now extinct, but their relatives live on – and they might be quite familiar to you!

Fossils such as this tell us what the ancestors of today's animals looked like.

In this book you'll find out about some amazing animal ancestors from long ago. You'll also find out about their closest living relatives. There is a size guide on each page, showing the animal ancestor next to an adult human. You may be surprised by the size of the animals!

Can you guess what the ancestors of these animals looked like?

THE IN-BETWEEN DOG

or Amphicyonid (say: am-fih-sy-o-nid)

Another name for the in-between dog is the bear-dog, because it's an ancestor of both bears and dogs. Bear-dogs lived across Asia and North America until about nine million years ago.

Scientists have found footprint fossils, which show that the bear-dog walked like bears do now. It moved its two left legs together first, then the two right legs.

The bear-dog lived in underground dens and fed on smaller animals. It was a strong digger, and could burrow after its prey.

Closest living relatives: bear and dog

4

How big was it?

THE ARGENTINE BIRD

or *Argentavis (say: ar-jen-tay-vis)*

The remains of this huge bird were found in Argentina, in South America. It lived there until about five million years ago.

It was the largest ever flying bird. It was about five feet tall, with wings that measured 25 feet across. Each wing feather could be as long as five feet.

This ancient bird ate small animals such as lizards, mice, and rabbits. It also ate fish.

Closest living relatives: stork and vulture

How big was it?

THE INDRIK BEAST

or *Indricotherium (say: in-dreek-oh-thair-ee-um)*

This animal lived in Asia about 30 million years ago. It was the largest ever mammal to walk on land.

The very biggest of these creatures grew to about 15 feet tall. It had a long neck that made it even taller, so that it could reach leaves high up in the trees.

It was also a very heavy animal. A really big one weighed 33,000 pounds – that's much heavier than the largest rhino!

Closest living relative: rhinoceros

How big was it?

THE EARTH MOLE

or Mammoth (say: mam-uth)

People used to believe that this animal was a giant that lived underground and died when it saw daylight. However, we now know that the mammoth was a type of large elephant.

The bones of mammoths have often been found half-buried in frozen parts of the world, but they actually lived in many different places. Those that lived in cold countries had long fur to keep them warm.

Mammoths grew up to 10 feet tall, and ate mostly grass and bushes. They had two long tusks that they used to protect themselves from attackers.

Closest living relative:
elephant

How big was it?

THE MIDDLE HORSE

or Mesohippus (say: mez-oh-hip-us)

About 40 million years ago, this small, dog-sized animal grew to look like a little horse. However, unlike a horse, it didn't have hooves on its feet. Instead, it had three toes on each foot.

It was only about 20 inches tall, but it had long legs. This meant that it could run fast and escape from saber-toothed cats and other meat-eating animals.

This shy little animal ate only fruit and leaves.

Closest living relative: horse

How big was it?

THE PAKISTAN WHALE

or *Pakicetus (say: pak-ee-see-tus)*

Fossils of this animal have been found in Pakistan. They are 54 million years old.

This ancient creature is an ancestor of the whale. It had legs instead of flippers, so it could walk on land. It also had nostrils at the end of its snout, rather than a blowhole on the top of its head.

This animal was a meat-eater, and probably hunted fish and other small mammals that lived in or near water.

Closest living relative: whale

How big was it?

THE GIANT SHORT-FACED KANGAROO

or Procoptodon (say: proh-kop-toe-don)

This animal lived in Australia until about 50,000 years ago. It weighed up to 450 pounds – that's more than twice as heavy as today's biggest kangaroo.

Each of the creature's hind feet had one single large claw, like a hoof. Its long arms could stretch up over its head, and its long, grabbing "fingers" could reach leaves high up on trees. It was able to chew really tough leaves with its strong jaw.

Closest living relative: kangaroo

How big was it?

17

THE SABER TOOTH

or Smilodon (say: smy-loh-don)

Another name for the smilodon is the saber-toothed cat. Many well-preserved fossil skeletons of these creatures have been found in California.

The saber-toothed cat was very fierce. It had two long, sword-shaped teeth that it used to kill its prey. It could open its mouth very wide – almost twice as wide as a lion.

It had short, sturdy legs and a very short tail. It couldn't run very fast, so it probably hid, and then pounced on its prey.

Closest living relative: lion

How big was it?

THE TERROR BIRD

or *Titanis (say: tee-tawn-is)*

This giant bird lived about two million years ago in North America. It couldn't fly because it didn't have wings, but it did have arms covered in feathers.

This bird stood nearly 10 feet tall, and could run very fast. It was a meat-eater, and hunted small animals using its sharp claws and very large beak to grip and kill them.

Closest living relative: moorhen

How big was it?

ANIMAL ANCESTORS

walked like a bear	largest ever flying bird	had a long neck	had fur to keep it warm	only 20 inches tall
lived in an underground den	ate small animals	weighed 33,000 lbs.	had tusks to protect it	ate fruit and leaves

| could walk on land | had a long claw on each hind foot | had two long teeth | couldn't fly |

| was a meat-eater | had long fingers | had short sturdy legs | ate small animals |

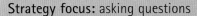 Ideas for Guided Reading

Strategy focus: asking questions

Skills that could be addressed:
- Scanning a text to find specific sections
- Skimming title and table of contents to find out what a book may be about
- Building new words from reading linked to particular topics

Curriculum links: science (variation, animal families, plants and animals in the local environment)

Word count: 964

Getting started – introducing the book

This book may be read over two sessions.

- Have the students look at the table of contents. Then have them turn each chapter title into a question and generate questions they have before reading. Make note of the questions students have.

- Explain to the students that they will be using the strategy of "asking questions" to help them better understand this text. Ask how this might help them as readers.

Reading and responding

- Ask the students to silently read pp. 2–3, thinking about the question they used for the title and focusing on questions they have while reading.

- After reading, encourage the students to discuss their new questions, and how starting with a question helped their reading. Ask the students to discuss how the question on p. 3 helped their thinking. Make note of new questions.